FORCE

A CHOREOPOEM

Small Harbor Publishing

Cover art: Steve Gibson
Cover design: Hercules Platts
Interior design: Brianna Chapman
Editor: Beth Bolton
Publisher: Allison Blevins
Executive Editor: Kristiane Weeks-Rogers
Managing Editor: Bianca Dagostino

FORCE: A CHOREOPOEM
MONICA PRINCE
ISBN 978-1-957248-61-5
Harbor Editions,
an imprint of Small Harbor Publishing

FORCE

A CHOREOPOEM

Monica Prince

Harbor Editions
Small Harbor Publishing

for every Black girl who can't say her name out loud

Contents

FORCE

A CHOREOPOEM

DRAMATIS PERSONAE

VICTIM – Black woman wearing a loose wrinkled black dress who mostly speaks in fragments.

SURVIVOR – Black woman wearing a pressed blue dress with pockets who speaks mostly grammatically correct English.

WHORE – Black woman wearing a sexy form-fitting purple dress who speaks casually.

RAPE FANTASY – Woman of color wearing a red scandalous outfit.

RAPISTS (3) – Men of any race wearing colors matching their prey (cannot also play LOVERS).

LOVERS (3) – Men of any race wearing colors matching their prey (cannot also play RAPISTS).

PTSD, DEPRESSION, SUICIDAL IDEATION, & WHORE'S BODY – People of color wearing red shirts and black leggings or sweatpants (can be played by RAPISTS, LOVERS, or DANCERS).

DANCERS (min.: 6) – People of any race (people of color preferred) wearing black shirts and black leggings or sweatpants (can also play RAPISTS, LOVERS, PTSD, DEPRESSION, SUICIDAL IDEATION, and WHORE'S BODY).

Blackout. Overlapping voices slowly come over the speakers, repeating various lines from the choreopoem. Dancers enter the room from all sides, poking and prodding at audience members, hissing and growling. Crawling and creeping, they move on and off the stage, between and around seats. The voices get louder and more distinctive over the speakers. The dancers shift direction and move toward the stage, collapsing in different poses as the voices reach a definitive crescendo and render themselves silent. Beat.

VICTIM *(offstage)*
i do not have a name

SURVIVOR *(offstage)*
My name does not matter.

RAPE FANTASY *(offstage)*
You hesitate to name me.

WHORE *(offstage)*
if you knew it, what would you call me?

Victim, Survivor, Rape Fantasy, and Whore repeat their lines as the dancers struggle to their feet. They lean on each other and pick one another up. Victim, Survivor,

*Rape Fantasy, and Whore
stop speaking when all the
dancers stand. Beat.*

SURVIVOR *(offstage)*
He said I deserved it.

WHORE *(offstage)*
she told me i was a slut.

VICTIM *(offstage)*
they all called me a liar

*Victim, Survivor, Whore, and
Rape Fantasy repeat "liar" at
different speeds and with
different inflections, causing the
dancers to twitch, jerk, and
shake. They all grab their
heads, shoulders, and
abdomens and scream,
stopping the voices. After a few
beats of silence, the dancers
straighten themselves and stand
still. As the lights slowly come
up, two dancers leave the stage
and return carrying Victim.
They dump her at the front of
the stage and return to their
places.*

VICTIM
they call me victim

*Survivor walks on stage and
stands next to Victim.*

SURVIVOR
A survivor.

*Whore crawls from offstage
and deposits herself on the
ground next to Survivor,
refusing to touch her.*

WHORE
a whore.

*As the three speak, dancers
begin a synchronized dance.*

VICTIM
i didn't start out like this

SURVIVOR
Never wanted to be this way.

WHORE
nicer labels do exist.

VICTIM
so do nicer people

SURVIVOR
Who gave you this title?

WHORE
who took your name?

SURVIVOR
Can you remember how it's spelled?

WHORE
do you want to be someone else?

9

VICTIM
does it matter

WHORE
do you want to know a secret?

ALL
We like it.

> *Beat. Victim and Whore*
> *stand, and everyone joins the*
> *dancers in their dance.*

SURVIVOR
Anyone can get used to anything.

VICTIM
play the role long enough

WHORE
& it becomes second nature.

SURVIVOR
Like riding a bike,

VICTIM
a bike of shame/ disappointment   & regret

WHORE
even in this regret,

ALL
we'll never apologize,

WHORE
act differently,

VICTIM
change our tune

SURVIVOR
break the habit.

ALL
Instead—

SURVIVOR
We'll say thank you for the compliment.

WHORE
offer tips on how to be just like us.

VICTIM
kiss your cheek/ say we understand

ALL
We do.

VICTIM
what's a little addiction between friends

Dance ends.

DANCERS
Tell me you love me.

Dancers scatter through the
audience and off stage.

VICTIM
cunt is shorter/ but not sweeter

SURVIVOR
Vagina sounds too clinical.

WHORE
box lacks creative flair.

VICTIM
one lover called it my *lady curtains*/
but isn't that just sexist

WHORE
i'm searching for a word that includes
both sets of labia, vagina, mons, & buzzing
clitoris (not to forget the quiet cervix
for its occasional contribution to the orgasm),

SURVIVOR
one word that encompasses the whole region
of feminine power. I want to write a poem for her,
a qasida for her grace and zeal,
this sacred bowl worthy of yielding
all control.

VICTIM
i'm trying not to project
my ignorance onto her—
          who hasn't stared between her own thighs
          in the mirror/   folds opening & winking

WHORE
if i'm to come into my erotic power,
excising negativity might be the only way.

SURVIVOR
I want the following: touch, truth,
temptation, belonging, excitement,

divinity, riot, joy, kinetic qi flowing
from one being to another.

VICTIM
i want to reach down with 1 licked finger
/or 2/ rub a circle on the upper left
/my left/ quadrant of my vibrating zenith
my sex/ join one more
repeat

WHORE
until all available pleasure, wrung
from these nerves with precision & impatience,
flows unbidden.

SURVIVOR
I coax each wave jolting wet thighs,
the following quivers

VICTIM
enough to forget the word i was looking for

WHORE
before i decided to masturbate.

> *Blackout. The dancers exit the*
> *space with Survivor and*
> *Whore.*

RAPIST 1 *(offstage)*
Let's play a game.

> *Lights up. Dancers enter with*
> *a bed, a bottle of vodka, shot*
> *glasses, and a remote control.*
> *They move Victim and place*
> *her on the bed. She perks up.*

Rapist 1 enters.

RAPIST 1
Let's play a game.

VICTIM
what kind

RAPIST 1
A drinking game.

Rapist 1 freezes.

VICTIM *(to the audience)*
i'm 18/ he's 21
he's been trying to get me into his room
since i was 17/ under the guise/
skin folk are your kin folk
no one has told me yet
this is not true

Rapist 1 unfreezes and sits on the bed. He pours them both shots.

RAPIST 1
Have you ever heard "Roxanne"? By The Police?

VICTIM
no

They both take their shots. Rapist 1 grabs the remote and moves closer to Victim. He cues the song. "Roxanne" by The Police begins to play softly over the speakers.

RAPIST 1
Every time they sing, "Roxanne," you drink.
Every time they say, "Put on the red light," I'll drink.

> *Rapist 1 pours them another shot and they start the game. Victim gets visibly tipsy very quickly. Rapist 1 foregoes pouring the shots and they start to pass the bottle back and forth. Around the second chorus, Victim pushes the bottle away. Rapist 1 continues drinking, rubbing Victim and trying to get her to drink. Victim turns to the audience.*

VICTIM
they say /roxanne/ 26 times

RAPIST 1
Come on, you're behind!

VICTIM
/put on the red light/ 25 times

RAPIST 1
You better take a long shot to catch up.

> *Victim takes a long drink of the bottle as the song fades out, coughing and spitting at the burn.*

RAPIST 1
Perfect.

VICTIM *(to the audience)*
this is the last time i drink vodka
the last time i play a rigged drinking game
on an empty stomach
(slurring) the last thing i remember—

RAPIST 1
You good, baby?

VICTIM *(slurring)*
before—

RAPIST 1 *(removing her clothes)*
You're getting hot. Take this off.

VICTIM *(slurring)*
the lights—

RAPIST 1
You're so sexy.

VICTIM *(slurring)*
go out

> *Lights change and flash as Victim and Rapist 1 struggle on the bed. Finally, she passes out. Rapist 1 takes off his shirt and looms over her. Lights dim. Sounds of movement are heard, ending with a deep groan from Rapist 1. Beat. Rapist 1 lies down on the bed next to Victim. Lights come up. Victim wakes up, looks around in horror, then*

stumbles to her feet.

VICTIM
this is the moment/
                    when i stop being me
become
victim

> *Lights flash and sputter while*
> *"El Tango de Roxanne" by*
> *Ewan McGregor, Jacek*
> *Koman, and José Feliciano*
> *plays softly. Victim puts on*
> *her clothes.*

VICTIM
i went home/ he went home
i showered/ he showered
i called rape/ he called slut
i became a statistic/ & he   /.../
well   /.../   he became a father
a school superintendent
a supreme court justice
a president

> *Now dressed, Victim begins to*
> *dance a violent lyrical dance,*
> *mimicking a panic attack.*

VICTIM
consider this the report i didn't file
the shower i shouldn't have taken
the cop i didn't call
the charges i didn't press
the violence i didn't use
to end his life—

consider this the moment
where i turn victim
& he turns victor

consider this the reason
i don't make the transition—
i can't protect myself
without protecting him

if i say his name
the next moment
will just be rape
again & again—
my credibility
only as good
as the integrity
of my hymen

*Victim's dance ends and she
collapses on the floor. Music
gets louder. Dancers enter with
a full-length standing mirror
and remove the bottle, glasses,
and remote, repositioning the
bed while Rapist 1 exits. They
pull Victim to her feet, who
appears catatonic, and remove
her outer layer. On the back
wall of the stage, the word
"RAPE" is projected.
Survivor enters and watches.
The lights stabilize but
continue to flash at odd
intervals. The song decreases in
volume and eventually stops.*

As the poem progresses,
dancers use markers, lipstick,
or eye/lip liner to write
"RAPE" all over Victim's
body.

SURVIVOR
Shock—associated meanings have little
to do with violation. Obviously legal
definitions, Latin cognates, uses
dating back half a millennium,
but don't expect justice—any evidence
of education as an equalizing concept.

Other definitions include, to no surprise:
to plunder, or to seize, remove by force.
Sex omitted, focused only on missing consent.
Only on power. Still, we each prove simple lessons,
innocent symbols killed to justify
future quests into territory uninvited.

A rare definition, often discounted:
the residue leftover from transforming hydrated raisins
into wine, the base for fixing vinegar. The French word
for "sour wine." Dictionaries know nothing of taste,
offering etymology trails instead of solutions,
how to judge disaster or consequences
from such lazy connections. Vinegar
feels almost like betrayal, but not quite.

Soaking colorful fabrics in this concoction
prior to washing maintains vibrancy to guard ivory thongs
and snowy shirts. A small comfort, though
lacking in application for acquiring a tabula rasa
following trauma. July will still burn bloody in mind,
maximizing scars on an amygdala too soggy with panic.
Insomnia nights pass. Months pass without touch.

19

A song causing involuntary flashbacks.
A dictionary knows nothing of stasis,
a body starving, a brain drowning in guilt mislaid.
Say *assault*, say *attack*, say all but what it is:
an action, a sin, a tomb.

> *Lights stabilize and stop flashing. Dancers all exit quietly, leaving a marker in Victim's hands. She comes to and starts coughing. She looks at herself in the mirror, sees the marker in her hand, and realizes what has happened. She grabs her clothes from the floor and frantically dresses.*

SURVIVOR
Hey.

VICTIM *(defeated, turning to the voice)*
oh/ hey

SURVIVOR
Are you okay?

VICTIM *(smiling weakly, arms crossed, nodding)*
yeah/ sure

> *Survivor crosses the stage to Victim, who moves away from her. Cautiously, Survivor approaches Victim again, and lifts Victim's sleeve. The words, now smeared but still visible, make Survivor sigh heavily. Victim pulls away,*

ashamed and uncomfortable.

SURVIVOR
Who did this to you?

VICTIM
me

SURVIVOR
No. No, you didn't.

> *Victim takes a few beats to
> compose herself and process
> what Survivor said. She looks
> at Survivor.*

VICTIM
what/   how do you know

SURVIVOR
Oh, beloved—that's not your handwriting.

> *Victim examines the words on
> her body more carefully,
> looking in the mirror. Soon,
> she picks up the mirror and
> throws it offstage. She looks
> back at Survivor.*

SURVIVOR
Who did this to you?

> *Beat.*

VICTIM *(to audience)*
even though the phrase/ *i was raped* / is passive

21

i promise/ it's very active
passive voice indicates
a lack of agency

SURVIVOR
But not this time.

*Survivor takes off her outer
layer to reveal "rape" written
all over her own body. Victim
gasps.*

SURVIVOR
Don't forget—

VICTIM
i'm the protagonist

SURVIVOR
I survive.

*Dancers enter carrying two
large wash tubs, washcloths,
and bonnets. Survivor puts
Victim's hair in a bonnet and
Victim does the same for her.
The dancers help each of them
get in the tubs; others take
their old clothes offstage and
bring new ones that they
smooth on the bed. During the
poem, dancers scrub the words
from Victim and Survivor's
bodies. Survivor and Victim
keep their eyes closed for most
of the poem, visibly relaxing as*

the dancers care for them. As the poem ends, dancers towel dry Victim and Survivor's skin and help them redress.

DANCERS
sacred sex

DANCER 1
love the love, the happy,
the drunken, the bad

DANCER 2
love the power,
the waiting

DANCERS
what feels good?

DANCER 3
expand—keep taking things
to the next level
& we all suffer

DANCER 4
sometimes sex heals us

DANCERS
sometimes sex heals us

DANCER 5
going wild is freeing
restraint isn't always restrictive

DANCER 6
rather, own that inhibition, that intimacy

embrace your natural cravings for love & acceptance

DANCER 1
learn to say *no*
so you can say *yes*

DANCERS
a sacred emptying

DANCER 2
you did not do this to yourself,
so desperate for attention

DANCERS
what feels good?

DANCER 3
sex is the most direct route to spiritual liberation

DANCER 4
guide it up the spine

DANCER 5
find the cosmos in a properly handled orgasm

DANCER 6
reach nirvana this way

DANCERS
reach forgiveness

DANCER 1
you are a crucial power source for miracles

DANCER 2
sex a spiritual container—
desire the first ingredient in a healing potion

DANCER 3
you want to be fucked open to God

DANCERS
you want to be fucked open to God
you want to be fucked open to God

DANCER 4
your communion as service
to save your own life

DANCER 5
this deep devotion is worth holding on to,
wildly so

DANCER 6
pleasure is power

DANCERS
pleasure is power

DANCER 1
what feels good?
how will you live now?

DANCERS
how will you live now?
how will you live now?
how will you live now?

Dancers finish dressing
Survivor and Victim, then

*exit with the bathing
materials. Victim and
Survivor look at one another,
hold hands and embrace.
Victim gets into bed and
sleeps.*

SURVIVOR

I think we forget that there is an *after* after the violence. A *post* hyphenated to the traumatic. Whoever is left alive must go to work, pay bills, cook lunch, take the dog for a walk.

In that loneliness, I remember—the cost of loving others is their capacity for cruelty. It could be anyone. It could happen anywhere. To ask for sweetness is to assume poison lurks in their pockets. No one is immune.

Dancer 6 enters.

DANCER 6

Some of the behaviors a sexual assault survivor may exhibit include but are not limited to flashbacks, panic attacks, loss of sexual appetite, increased or compulsory sexual behavior, depression, anxiety, substance abuse, paranoia, rape fantasies, post-traumatic stress, self-harm, eating disorders, hypervigilance, and suicidal ideation.

*Dancer 6 exits. Survivor goes
to the edge of the stage and sits
down. An instrumental song
plays. She begins a languid
dance that happens mostly on
the ground, similar to a yin
yoga routine. Dancers enter
and exit as they say lines,
joining Survivor's dance for*

DANCER 1
requesting proof

DANCER 2
a slap in the face

SURVIVOR
How dare you?
Given so much history

DANCER 3
evidence

DANCER 4
you want more?

DANCER 5
lie detector malfunctioned

DANCER 1
judge of character

DANCER 2
gut

DANCER 3
who deserves

DANCER 4
to be believed

SURVIVOR
by default?

DANCERS
better plan:

SURVIVOR
I tell the story again
with eye contact.

DANCER 5
record every time

DANCER 1
he flinches

DANCERS
then/

SURVIVOR
will you call it rape?

DANCERS
then/

DANCER 2
will you ask him

DANCER 3
to prove himself

SURVIVOR
innocent?

Beat.

DANCER 4
repeat until it stops

DANCER 5
boring holes

DANCER 1
into my sternum:

DANCERS *(popcorn-style, using different inflections)*
rape / rape / rape / rape
rape / rape / rape
rape / rape
rape

> *Beat. Victim starts thrashing
> in bed, a night terror accosting
> her subconscious.*

ALL
believe me—

SURVIVOR
I'm tired
of telling the truth.

> *Song and dance end abruptly.
> Dancers exit as the lights flash
> and sputter. Soon, Victim
> wakes herself screaming.
> Lights settle. After a few
> beats, she calms down.*

VICTIM
a nightmare

SURVIVOR
What was it this time?

VICTIM
i saw   her

SURVIVOR
Her?

VICTIM
she   /.../   she   /.../

SURVIVOR
Oh, you don't mean—

RAPE FANTASY *(offstage)*
Say my name.

> *Rape Fantasy walks on stage.*
> *Victim trembles at her*
> *presence. Survivor scoots across*
> *the stage opposite Victim.*
> *Rape Fantasy stands center*
> *and considers them.*

RAPE FANTASY
Tell them who I am.

> *Victim refuses to make eye*
> *contact with her as Survivor*
> *tries to steel herself. Rape*
> *Fantasy rolls her eyes and*
> *starts filing her nails, pacing*
> *across the stage.*

VICTIM
i wake in damp sheets/ my vibrator
dead/ the windows open

you perch
on the radiator
filing your nails
to sharp points

SURVIVOR
It feels dangerous to breathe,
even ask your name.

VICTIM
no eye contact

SURVIVOR
You tell me—

RAPE FANTASY
Took you long enough.

SURVIVOR
My conversations with you
are reluctant, hostile. I don't like
spending time with you in early afternoons
like this one—sunlight blocked by gray
clouds, hardly anyone outside.

VICTIM
it's here you find me
break into my bedroom
guide my hand
between my legs

SURVIVOR
whisper—

RAPE FANTASY
You know you want to.

VICTIM
i haven't learned what to call you yet

SURVIVOR
To admit you exist corporeally.

VICTIM
any confession makes you real
not a hallucination

SURVIVOR
or a side effect from too many pills,
too much smoke, not enough sleep.

Victim tries to cover herself.

SURVIVOR
I gather bedclothes around me,
and that's when you pounce, rip them
from my grasp, cackle—

RAPE FANTASY *(sitting on the bed, playing with Victim)*
Really? Shame? This late in the game?

VICTIM
it's not a game   to me

SURVIVOR
Knowing you are a thief of my orgasms,
that I can never call myself survivor

VICTIM
when you make me victim

SURVIVOR
I hate that you look like me—same hands,
same hair—but sexier, more alluring,
your lips a constant invitation.

VICTIM & SURVIVOR
I hate how much I love you,
want to be you,

SURVIVOR
want to give in to the reckless abandon
being raped has created in me.
Finally, you say—

RAPE FANTASY *(turning toward Survivor)*
Call me by the right name.

VICTIM
i can't utter it   out loud

> *Rape Fantasy leaves Victim in*
> *bed and closes in on Survivor,*
> *miming the following lines.*

VICTIM
you wrap a hand around my neck
pull me to your face
insist on eye contact
to reveal what you've made me/
submissive   passive   frantic to be forced
coerced

tricked
deceived
hurt

SURVIVOR
punished.

RAPE FANTASY
Say it!

VICTIM & SURVIVOR *(resigned)*
Rape Fantasy.

> *Rape Fantasy pulls Survivor*
> *to her feet and they dance.*
> *Victim remains cowering in*
> *bed, focused on the pair.*

SURVIVOR
Deeper than the desire to be dominated.
No—ultimately, subs have all the control,
the permission to stop everything.

VICTIM
you are not that—
you are carnal need
for attention   irreparable abuse   unfathomed harm

SURVIVOR
I crave unbridled suffering

VICTIM
molestation on public transit

SURVIVOR
waking up in a stranger's car,
his cock already inside me

VICTIM
an acquaintance calls me a tease
one moment
jams my own panties
down my throat &
fucks me in the ass
the next

*Rape Fantasy tosses Survivor
toward the bed. Victim grabs
her and holds her. Rape
Fantasy begins dancing alone,
drunk on her own power. She
alternates between caressing
Victim and Survivor and
dancing across the stage.*

SURVIVOR
I wish I could conjure shame,
but you've turned comfortable, warm.
You curl around me in the covers,
purr in my ear, lazily stroke
my labia, recently waxed,
just in case.

VICTIM
i don't fight anymore

SURVIVOR
I used to, in the beginning,
when you'd interrupt a normal train of thought
with your bombastic presence.

I don't fight anymore—

VICTIM
when you walk me down empty streets
alone & drunk
flirting with a dangerous man
daring him
to follow me home

VICTIM & SURVIVOR
I don't fight anymore.

SURVIVOR
I used to cry when you disappeared in favor
of the real thing, an actual rape—my face in his lap,
his dick rising to meet my lips, a heavy grip
on the back of my head. In the beginning,
I preferred you to the come-true—at least then,
there were no bruises or cum to floss out
from between my teeth.

RAPE FANTASY
And now?

VICTIM
now/   you're tattooed on my thigh

SURVIVOR
I catch glimpses of you in red lipstick,
knee-high boots, a low-cut blouse.

VICTIM
you appear in the way i hold my pen
apply lotion
craft sentences on my tongue

SURVIVOR
I want you the way I want proof
this is normal, completely acceptable,
nothing alarming.

VICTIM
i want you like
i want *them* to want me/

ALL
violently.

SURVIVOR
I want you how I want the orgasm
you edge me toward, fervently now,

VICTIM
maniacally

SURVIVOR
without apology
or care for open windows.

*Rape Fantasy cackles and
tumbles into the bed with
Victim and Survivor. Victim
sobs while Survivor clings to
Rape Fantasy. Soon, Rapist 2
enters, holding hands with
Whore. Rape Fantasy leaves
the bed and lurks upstage as
the poem progresses. Whore
and Rapist 2 circle one
another, Rapist 2 constantly
pulling Whore into his arms.*

RAPIST 2
It's simple.

WHORE
you say i'm cold, call me
unpatriotic
if i don't just do it.

RAPIST 2
Don't you know your citizenship
is tied to your sexual loyalty
to those who sacrifice themselves
for this country?

WHORE
like i don't know sacrifice—
the name of the closest air force base,
the pledge of allegiance stamped in my memory.

RAPIST 2
I've been honorably discharged.
I served my country, did *my* duty
for *your* freedom.

WHORE
freedom, huh?

RAPIST 2
You should be grateful.

WHORE
who told you about dismemberment?
splitting a body in two
using your bare hands—only the practiced
pull that off, the ones who paid attention
in training.

38

An instrumental heavy metal version of "The Star-Spangled Banner" plays. Rapist 2 grabs Whore from behind, claps a hand over her mouth, and forces her to the ground. He pins her hands above her head, flips her onto her back, and looms over her.

WHORE
in war, rape is a tactical strategy—your penis
now a weapon, an assault rifle, a sniper.

RAPIST 2
I have twelve confirmed kills.

WHORE
which anthem should i belt out?
what part of the constitution?
can a body self-combust like an IED?

RAPIST 2
You should thank me for my service.

WHORE
don't you mean treason?

Rapist 2 hears this and goes to slap Whore. The lights go out and the song stops. Rapist 2 exits. The lights return and Whore lies on the ground breathing heavily. Rape Fantasy helps Whore to her feet. Suicidal Ideation, PTSD, and Depression enter. Rape Fantasy exits. Spiritual music begins as Victim, Survivor, and Whore space out on the stage. Suicidal Ideation, PTSD, and Depression perform a praise dance in the center of the stage.

ALL *(singing)*
Gonna hold my head up high
Gonna hold my head up high
When my Lord come take me
Gonna hold my head up high

VICTIM *(singing)*
i down pills like candy
i know how many will end me
lord/ how you gon' save me
wash 'em down/ go sweetly

SURVIVOR *(singing)*
Blade clean enough for cuttin'
Sharp enough I won't feel nothin'
Need to prove I'm somethin'
More than a body made for cuffin'

ALL *(singing)*
Gonna hold my head up high
Gonna hold my head up high
When my Lord come take me
Gonna hold my head up high

WHORE *(singing)*
water & spark just don't mix
come together to bark & hiss

in this body is where they'll kiss
stop my heart & give me bliss

SURVIVOR *(singing)*
Loaded gun, a steel revolver
Ain't scared of the hereafter
Easy to finish with a trigger
So tired of havin' to be stronger

ALL *(singing)*
Gonna hold my head up high
Gonna hold my head up high
When my Lord come take me
Gonna hold my head up high

VICTIM *(singing)*
on a bridge, no fear of heights
up so high to attempt flight
where you at/ lord/ show your might
show me i'm worthy of this life

WHORE *(singing)*
when sinking at so low a depth
they say to just take a deep breath
a waste of a life, really a theft
fighting to erase all that's left

Singing and dancing stop but
music continues softly.

SURVIVOR
Folks believe Black women don't kill themselves

WHORE
because we have so much to fight for.

VICTIM
but when even our bodies betray us

ALL
What are we supposed to live for?

Beat.

ALL *(singing)*
Gonna hold my head up high
Gonna hold my head up high
When my Lord come take me
Gonna hold my head up high...

*Music fades softly as the song
ends. Suicidal Ideation,
PTSD, and Depression go to
Victim, Survivor, and Whore,
respectively, and push them to
their knees. As they taunt
their partners, Victim,
Survivor, and Whore go back
and forth between resignation
and defiance.*

VICTIM
eject me from this earth
this can't happen again

SUICIDAL IDEATION
it would be so easy
to die

SURVIVOR
It's not a problem
until you have a plan.

42

WHORE
otherwise, it's just a wish.

PTSD
What if he didn't stop,
brought his friends to join in?

DEPRESSION
let's stay in bed today.
no shower. no food.

VICTIM
will it happen again

SURVIVOR & WHORE
Yes.

SUICIDAL IDEATION
no one will care when you're gone

SURVIVOR
Maybe next time, I'll press charges.

PTSD
That guy looks just like your ex.

WHORE
maybe next time, i won't fuck him again.

DEPRESSION
is any of this worth it?

VICTIM
maybe next time—

PTSD
What's that sound?

SURVIVOR
Maybe next time—

DEPRESSION
do the laundry tomorrow

SURVIVOR & WHORE
Maybe next time—

SUICIDAL IDEATION
let's take a bath with your favorite
paring knife

VICTIM
maybe next time—

PTSD
Take a sedative to sleep.

DEPRESSION
but don't take too many.

VICTIM, SURVIVOR, & WHORE
Maybe next time—

SUICIDAL IDEATION
wouldn't want you to
never wake up
would we

VICTIM
maybe next time
                    they'll kill me

> *Victim, Survivor, and Whore*
> *slam their hands on the stage*
> *and look at the audience.*

Slowly, they turn and look at their respective tormentors.

WHORE
not yet.

VICTIM
not today

SURVIVOR
Not ever.

DANCER *(offstage)*
I ain't done yet.

At this sound, Victim, Survivor, and Whore fight and wrestle Suicidal Ideation, PTSD, and Depression to the ground. Other dancers enter and help drag the symptoms off stage. Breathing heavily, Victim, Survivor, and Whore high-five and hug. Dancers bring out the full-length mirror again, slightly cracked. Survivor and Victim go to bed while Whore adjusts her appearance in the mirror. Whore's Body enters.

WHORE'S BODY
survivors of sexual assault may learn to use sex as a coping mechanism for negative feelings, or as a strategy to avoid other potential forms of harm. this leads many to be sexually trafficked due to their increased vulnerability and impaired ability to register danger. other

45

survivors may willingly enter sex work, or "THE LIFE," to
validate the potential belief that their bodies are only
good for sex—

WHORE
so i might as well get paid for it.

> *Dancers remove the mirror.*
> *Whore's Body begins mirroring*
> *Whore's movements, eventually*
> *dancing with her. As Whore*
> *recites, she becomes increasingly*
> *aware of Whore's Body and*
> *begins addressing her directly.*

WHORE
the temptation of THE LIFE calls louder
than other kinds. i can easily ignore
urges for fast food, a second bottle of wine,
or texting an ex while lonely,
but i can't control THE LIFE's cunning
efforts to make me return.

when i first started, yes, i'll admit—
it was empowering, intoxicating, electrifying.
having a secret of that magnitude
gave me focus, energy, protection. in the beginning,
it was the kind of addiction that prevented
eviction, starvation, & suicide attempts.

the problem with addiction is its slithering
into the bloodstream, how it binds with receptors
meant for other hormones & chemicals.
one moment, everything is under control; the next—
each encounter either validates or eviscerates
the belief that i am worthy of attention, nice things,

love. not healthy. i only got out after a client promised
cash for a sexy cleaning appointment, fucked me
to get a taste, & never paid me. not the first time
i'd been tricked, lied to, given nothing for something, but
it had to be the last. the secrets weren't fun anymore.
maybe they never were.

THE LIFE beckons fiercely. a dummy account
follows me to request my services as a sugar baby.

WHORE'S BODY
(always a scam.)

WHORE
an old man asks for my number
at a bank to teach me about *the world's oldest
profession*. someone on a dating app lists
findom as one of their kinks, & we match.

i've taken precautions, set up safeguards.
moved to a small town where everyone knows
everybody's business. raced past the adult shops
at top speed. deactivated & blocked & deleted
the profiles, accounts, erotic photos
from every device.

WHORE'S BODY
(including the cloud, just in case.)

WHORE
& yet, THE LIFE always finds a way. past due bills.
an empty pantry. a date's mind blown after
what i'd call mediocre sex. THE LIFE sends me a snap
& i nearly respond.

WHORE'S BODY
a stack of twenties on the nightstand.
anonymous gifts delivered to the house.
you fuck like a porn star slurred like a compliment.
every rapper's favorite to fuck
but never fight for.

Beat.

WHORE
no peace for a retired sex worker,
sobriety a daily battle.

*Whore stops moving and looks
directly at Whore's Body. She
goes to her and caresses her
cheek, then carefully holds
Whore's Body from behind.*

WHORE *(to Whore's Body)*
dear body—this is another attempt to apologize
for putting you in harm's way simply
by leaving the house or existing online.

dear body—you deserve better. temptation suffocates
my efforts—but i got us out. i got us out.
we won't go back again. we can't. let's celebrate
this tiny miracle every time we wake up unbound, free.

WHORE'S BODY
free, free, free…

*Whore and Whore's Body
sway together for a few beats,
then release each other.
Whore's Body exits as dancers
enter with two yoga mats then*

*exit. Survivor gets out of bed
and unfurls one yoga mat at
the front of the stage. Whore
takes her mat and rolls it
out facing Survivor's. Victim falls
asleep. As the poem progresses,
Survivor and Whore mirror
their yoga moves while reciting
to one another.*

WHORE
i struggle with my fantasies made reality, the
justification of it all. what happens if, next
time, shame never arrives, & i'm left with a man
who honors my consent to become a rag doll, to
give up control & leave agency to him? when the call
to stop's ignored & i don't care? what does that make me?
exactly what i've always been, perhaps, a
liar about my own pleasure? well, let's be frank: a whore
desperate to be dominated, climaxing from her chokes
& screams. hence, my struggle. am i still me
if i choose submission, but only in bed, while
the world outside believes me to be a proper fucking
adult without an ounce of violence in her? am i still me
if i choose who gets to use my own fantasy against
me & i choose incorrectly? i know it will happen again—a
stranger will turn fun into force, push my limits, the wall

SURVIVOR
of my comfort zone obliterated. Yes, I
know it will happen again. In the meantime, I beg
this man to only use his fingers, to make me crave him
like the oxygen not reaching my brain, to
spur me closer to release, safety be damned, any say
I may have in the matter ignored. I can't explain it.
I belong on my knees. Eyes and mouth open once again.

*Survivor and Whore end
holding each other's hands in
Warrior III. Dancer enters.*

DANCER
The next man to call me a *whore* chokes me while fucking
me against a wall. I beg him to say it again.

> *Lover 1, Lover 2, and Lover
> 3 enter. Dancer exits with yoga
> mats. Lover 2 and 3 help
> Survivor and Whore,
> respectively, come out of their
> poses and begin an intimate
> dance, a cross between a tango
> and dirty dancing. Lover 1
> coaxes Victim out of bed and
> guides her into a similar dance.*

WHORE
i'm not embarrassed about my carnal desire
to give control to a stranger, to allow
someone the dexterity of devour & lust
to force me into difficult zones of fear.

SURVIVOR
But I don't want to talk about it with you,

VICTIM
don't want your quiet judgement

WHORE
that's not so silent after all. i recoil from any
verdict stating imbalance in my qi for needing
scrapes on my palms, blood in my throat,
disrespecting jeers tossed against my back

as i collect my withered panties & torn
stockings. the risk, the wonder, the exit
from bright lights to dead-end streets—

SURVIVOR
all so I can imagine the hazy fantasy
of released blame.

VICTIM
i struggle to justify
why it feels like
i deserve to suffer

SURVIVOR
Why I crave a digit's attempt to touch wet
while observers watch. Why a quick forced
fuck amidst a crowded club makes
my sex grow, sizzle, hum.

VICTIM
you don't understand/ don't want to see
me reluctant/ slapped/ bowed

WHORE
you prefer consensual harm, my allowance
per your request. the body as subject
not object, as zealous & open—
that's sexy, not me reckless, hurt,
at the beck & call of a stranger
whose hands only value me degraded.

SURVIVOR
I cannot (will not?) explain conceded torture
to a lover. Unafraid of your reaction or recoil—
I'm more concerned with your potential invitation
to fulfill my dream (can we even call it that?
would nightmare be more appropriate?).

VICTIM
i fear your amazement/   then greed
at the option to revoke my approval
to render me nothing
more than joke
locker room talk/   after the blood

dries
                              stains

WHORE
i won't witness a beloved become
assailant. it's *my* fantasy. let's leave it so.

SURVIVOR
Pretend you never walked in on my dirty
expletives, fingers signing inside me, permission
to jump my bones in an alley, dark parking structure,
my own four walls. Alternatively,
please accept vanilla but amazing lovemaking,

VICTIM
languorous & consensual

WHORE
my sanction acquired graciously.
it's better,

SURVIVOR
I promise, if I say

ALL *(breathy)*
yes

VICTIM
instead of scream

ALL (*screaming*)
no.

> *At their scream, the Lovers*
> *back up. Slow R&B music*
> *plays. Dancers enter and clear*
> *the stage of all but the bed.*

WHORE
it's going to happen again.

SURVIVOR
Someone once said, the first time is the last time.

VICTIM
they never knew me

> *Whore twirls herself toward*
> *the bed and Victim follows.*
> *Rapist 3 enters and performs a*
> *lyrical dance with Survivor.*

SURVIVOR
Paintbrush in hand, my college art professor
asks us to paint a self-portrait—
one every week for the entire term.
Until I understand the assignment
(using a mirror and good lighting,
paint an *actual* portrait of your *actual* self)
and because I am a poet first and a painter
as a graduation requirement, I spend two hours
alone on a Monday night, painting
an afro filled with curls tinged black and auburn,
whipped like meringue. My body,
nearly absorbed by the hair I love so much,

is barely visible atop a yoga mat,
resolute in Warrior II.

What I'm trying to say is—
I see myself as larger than life,
my hair my crown, my body proof
of survival, the entire sky a royal reckoning.
My professor wants us to learn contour,
detail, shadow, shape—but I'm more
interested in suffering reclaimed
as strength, how blue tears after
another rape by a Black man I trusted
because he was Black mix with red blood
drawn out of the next Black man's throat
who tries it, my fingernails half-moon grips
on either side of his trachea,
trying to touch to snap.

This portrait is of myself,
I declare the following week, during critique,
while apologizing for not
understanding the assignment.
Upon revealing the canvas, clearly
marked with rage and triumph
and careful consideration of space,
my professor recognizes the attempt
to rewrite history—to have pressed charges
instead of returning a week later to hear:

RAPIST 3
I can't be with someone who's been with everyone.

SURVIVOR
—to have pressed charges instead of accepting

RAPIST 3
I'm gonna cum inside you!

54

SURVIVOR
—to have pressed charges instead of fighting back.

RAPIST 3
You're so sexy. I just couldn't help myself.

SURVIVOR
My professor points out
the expansion of my afro is a testimony
to my softness, how I struggle to maintain any
amidst the chaos of purple bruises
attempting to recolor my entire outlook on life.

I'm a poet first, so I know time travel only works
on the page—or, in this case, the canvas.
I want to crawl inside the paint,
become the unmovable 4C puff doing yoga
among black stars. But salvation requires pens
and brushes, wine and tears, time and space.
Did I say salvation? I think I meant a blank slate.

Rapist 3 exits.

VICTIM
why does it feel good

SURVIVOR
to have your power taken from you
by a stranger, by an acquaintance?

WHORE
it's not supposed to be like this.

Victim, Survivor, and Whore
come together and huddle on
the floor downstage. Rape

*Fantasy enters and watches
them. During the poem, she
pulls them apart, one by one,
and dances with them, but
when she releases them, they
return to the safety of each
other. Dancers enter and exit
the stage, representing other
fantasies, symptoms, lovers,
and rapists.*

RAPE FANTASY

You have always worn your fantasies
on your skin—but not around your wrists
or hung from your ear lobes.
Your fantasies stick to you like
prison tattoos, crude & beautiful,
loyalty worth the suffering of stolen pens
& makeshift needles. As a child,
you imagined a man would love you;
the older you got, the darker the image
on your heart grew. Other fantasies
are more fleeting: your first kiss, driving your car
into a lake, an acceptance speech
for your first Pulitzer. No laser removal necessary.
Those fantasies simply faded—you can
hardly see them anymore.

One fantasy took on a life of her own,
birthed from her cousin PTSD & your pathetic
lost self—me. I wasn't a tattoo—no, I was fertilized,
a being fed & stoked inside your womb
after yet another man raped you. I love
that word—*rape*—so named myself such.
Rape Fantasy—I found my own way
into your bloodstream, beelined
for your recovering brain. You didn't even know

I was there until you reclined for pleasure
& clutched an image: a public park, a stranger
with a knife, improvised ligatures around your wrists.
I pride myself on my vivacity. I dislike repetition,
always insistent on euphoria
even at the height of fear.

No one told you about me.

Experts listed the other symptoms that might appear—
Depression, Increased Sexual Appetite,
Anxiety, Reckless Behavior, PTSD, Sexual Anorexia,
Flashbacks, Nightmares, Suicidal Ideation—
& they each introduced themselves politely,
waited in the kitchen for their interviews.
Some stayed; some bought you a drink
at the bar but never stuck around for the toast; some
sent letters promising to call before their next visit.

But not me. I moved in, slept beside you
for years, reminded you that any person
who could replicate me was a criminal.
I told you, consent to my performances
could only happen between *us*—anything else
was assault, violation, another shower you shouldn't take.

& you leaned into me, eventually. Fantasies,
when fed a daily diet of masturbation & sex toys,
can overtake anyone. & who needs corporeal lovers
with videos playing in your head of what they could do,
given permission, when begged?

Years with me in your house, sweating in your sheets,
drinking the good wine, using up all
the hot water—you finally told someone about me.
A therapist prescribed "vanilla sex,"
the intention that maybe you'd learn to like it, learn

not to need me so much. But as with all bad remedies,
you preferred to never have sex again
than have boring sex.

I told you. It's better with me.

You'd learned shame from the Bible, from men
with gravelly throats, from mothers & sisters & friends
who'd learned it from fear. You started to fight
with me, blame me for symptoms I didn't create.

VICTIM *(shouting)*
i'm not supposed to want you!

SURVIVOR *(shouting)*
It's not supposed to be like this!

WHORE *(shouting)*
why can't i just be normal?!

RAPE FANTASY
I rolled my eyes, pulled you
back to bed, asked you
to say the safe word
once you saw stars.

Eviction notices were drafted but never sent.
No one followed up to see if I had moved out.

Honestly, you're not even supposed to talk about me.

> *Rape Fantasy slumps at the
> edge of the stage. Victim,
> Survivor, and Whore comfort
> her and slowly help her into
> bed during the next stanza.*

Once there, Victim, Survivor,
and Whore recite in a line at
the front of the stage.

VICTIM
i loved her—

                       i'll admit it

SURVIVOR
I loved her.

WHORE
i still do.

VICTIM
i didn't notice/ though
when she crawled out
from between my legs
to die

SURVIVOR
One should be more careful with her fantasies, and yet—
I looked up one day, months later,
and she wasn't where I left her.

WHORE
usually, i find Rape Fantasy
after a long day in a short skirt & tall boots—
she catches my attention
in the mirror as i pass
to clip my fingernails
or take the kettle off the burner.

VICTIM
sometimes/ she creeps up in a song played
at disrespectful decibels
while i clean the house

nude
push the vacuum across the carpet
scrub the bathroom sink with bleach

SURVIVOR
She takes me over, down, hard.

ALL
I can't stop her,

WHORE
don't want to, instead
open my mouth in praise,
blood blistering skin,
hips churning.

VICTIM
somehow/ months whispered by/   & i didn't notice
she was gone

SURVIVOR
I don't miss her—I don't miss
the way she would conjure men in dark clothes
with wild hands or rope, their mouths more insistent
than their own wanton need.

WHORE
i don't miss squeezing
my eyes tighter, tunneling into her, trying to find
her source & power, where she'd wrap me
in precipice & high wire.

VICTIM
i don't miss words she made shadows say
taking me against my will—*cunt*

SURVIVOR
bitch,

WHORE
whore.

…well. maybe i do miss that.

SURVIVOR
I should keep better track of my fantasies,
lest they leave me,
walk into oncoming traffic dry-eyed.

Rape Fantasy exits.

VICTIM
& yet/
when Rape Fantasy died
i didn't notice

SURVIVOR
Just one morning, all alone in my own bed,
I reached for her,

WHORE
& pulled back nothing.

VICTIM
i think she buried herself
in the backyard

SURVIVOR
became a series of yucca plants
planted around my first-floor windows.

WHORE
if she cannot live where she grew up, at least
she grows to shield me from what i always believed
i wanted—a stranger in my bedroom,

VICTIM
my tongue
tasting leather & thread

SURVIVOR
a knee in my back
the masked man promising me—

RAPE FANTASY *(offstage, hissing)*
you're gonna like it.

> *At the sound of Rape*
> *Fantasy's voice, Victim,*
> *Survivor, and Whore look*
> *toward the bed, realizing she's*
> *really gone. Dancers whirl*
> *around the stage, clearing it*
> *and moving Victim, Survivor,*
> *and Whore into the center.*
> *They keep moving as they ask*
> *questions.*

DANCER 1
Who are you?

DANCER 2
Who do you love?

DANCER 3
Where did you come from?

DANCER 4
How did you arrive?

DANCER 5
How will you begin?

DANCER 6
How will you live now?

DANCER 1
What is the shape of your body?

DANCER 2
Who is responsible for the suffering of your mother?

DANCER 3
What do you remember about the earth?

DANCER 4
What are the consequences of silence?

DANCER 5
Tell me what you know about dismemberment.

DANCER 6
Describe a morning you woke without fear.

DANCER 1
How will you prepare for your death?

DANCER 2
Have you prepared for your death?

DANCER 3
And what would you say if you could?

DANCERS
And what would you say if you could?
And what would you say if you could?
And what would you say if you could?

On the last repetition, the dancers stop in a circle around Victim, Survivor, and Whore. The women sit on the floor as the dancers follow, creating an open semicircle. They repeat the dance from the opening of the show, only seated.

DANCERS
And what would you say if you could?

VICTIM
i am not a graveyard

SURVIVOR
Not a series of open wounds.

WHORE
not an easy mark.

VICTIM
what would i say?

SURVIVOR
My name.

WHORE
my real name.

VICTIM
fashion my lips around each syllable

SURVIVOR
Tattoo it on my hands.

WHORE
what would i say?

VICTIM
to my body   i'm sorry

DANCERS
What would you say?

SURVIVOR
To my body, it's not fair.

DANCERS
What would you say?

WHORE
to my body—i forgive you.

SURVIVOR
What would I say?

VICTIM
i love you

WHORE
don't leave.

SURVIVOR
It's going to be okay.

ALL
The horizon doesn't lie.

WHORE
do not disrespect your creator

SURVIVOR
by removing yourself without permission.

DANCERS
And what would you say if you could?

VICTIM
i am not a victim

SURVIVOR
I am not a survivor.

WHORE
i am not a whore.

VICTIM
this body is holy ground

SURVIVOR
Believes in miracles.

WHORE
i will worship here.

ALL
I will worship here.
I will worship here.
I will worship here.

Dance ends. Everyone on stage
reaches out to the audience for
several beats.

VICTIM, SURVIVOR, & WHORE

I was always strong enough.
I am more than my wounds.
I must be greater than my survival.

*As they drop their arms,
everyone assumes a kneeling
position on their heels while
staring into the audience. The
following voice overs play
slowly, leaving a breath
between each one.*

RAPE FANTASY *(offstage)*
You contain multitudes, baby girl.

DANCER 1 *(voice over)*
Do not let this universe regret you.

DANCER 2 *(voice over)*
The body is not an apology.

DANCER 3 *(voice over)*
I know I'm going to disappoint somebody, but that
person can't be me.

DANCER 4 *(voice over)*
You are not invisible. You are not a problem. You are not
your illness.

DANCER 5 *(voice over)*
some of us know
we have never felt safe

DANCER 6 *(voice over)*
I hope you do not suffer.

RAPE FANTASY *(voice over)*
please, let me enter. please, let me leave whole.

DANCER 5 *(voice over)*
Every day that I exist I acknowledge that being alive is an act of resistance.

DANCER 6 *(voice over)*
Your silence will not protect you.

> *As the last voice echoes through the space, everyone places their hands on the floor and looks at the audience.*

DANCERS
What is your name?

VICTIM, SURVIVOR, & WHORE
Monica—

VICTIM
meaning advisor—

SURVIVOR
Wonderful Counselor—

WHORE
as in GOD.

> *Beat.*

RAPE FANTASY *(offstage)*
C'mon, Black girl.
Force yourself to live.

Dancers repeat the lines three times as everyone on stage slowly rises. Victim, Survivor, and Whore look at one another and hold hands at the edge of the stage. They smile for the first time, resolute in their decision.

VICTIM
i'm alive

SURVIVOR
Still alive.

WHORE
still fucking alive.

Dancers exit. Victim, Survivor, and Whore remain on stage. Lights out. All exit.

PRODUCTION NOTES, CHOREOPOEM NOTES, & ACKNOWLEDGEMENTS

Force is a choreopoem conceived in response to the included poem, "Rape Fantasy," written as part of The 5th Woman Fellowship & Stage Show in Oak Ridge, TN, in 2019. Directors should prioritize BIPOC performers when casting. The main characters—Victim, Survivor, Whore, and Rape Fantasy—must be cast as Black women or femme-centered/presenting people. Voice overs may be read by dancers with attributions included in the programs.

"The Beautiful Outlaw Praises the Pussy," "The Beautiful Outlaw Cries Rape," and "The Beautiful Outlaw Asks (Not) to Punish" are Oulipian constraints, specifically lipograms or "beautiful outlaws." This poetic form requires the writer to choose a word and match the number of stanzas to the number of letters in the word. Each stanza must omit its corresponding letter, while using the other twenty-five letters of the alphabet.

"fucked open to God" is a loose erasure poem using the text of "Chapter 12: Faux Freedoms: when sacred sex goes sideways" from *White Hot Truth* by Danielle LaPorte, reprinted with permission from the author.

"Golden Shovel for a Hypocrite" is a golden shovel, a poetic form created by Terrance Hayes in honor of Gwendolyn Brooks. The writer takes a poem, a phrase, or lines from songs or poems, and uses the words of their chosen quotation to end each line of the poem. In this golden shovel, the phrase is, "The next man to call me a *whore* chokes me while fucking me against a wall. I beg him to say it again," which comes from the chapter "Orange Peels" in Monica Prince's memoir, *Cures for Last Night's Leftovers: A Memoir of Polyamory & Gin*.

"And what would you say, if you could?" takes its title and the following questions within it from Bhanu Kapil's *The Vertical Interrogation of Strangers*.

The lines the dancers speak on pages 64-65 are cited as follows:

"You contain multitudes, baby girl." – a rephrase of Walt Whitman's line from "Song of Myself, 51"

"Do not let this universe regret you." – "Instructions for a Body" by Marty McConnell

"The body is not an apology." – "The Body Is Not an Apology" by Sonya Renee Taylor

"I know I'm going to disappoint somebody, but that person can't be me." – Lizz Huerta

"You are not invisible. You are not a problem. You are not your illness." – "Unfinished Letters from the Most Popular Kid in the Psych Ward" by Casey Rocheteau

"some of us know / we have never felt safe" – "September's Song, a Poem in Seven Days," specifically "4 Friday 9/14/01," by Lucille Clifton

"I hope you do not suffer." – "Love" by Matthew Dickman

"please, let me enter. please, let me leave whole." – "Lullaby for the Grieving" by Ashley M. Jones

"Every day that I exist I acknowledge that being alive is an act of resistance." – excerpt from *Field Study* by Chet'la Sebree

"Your silence will not protect you." – "The Transformation of Silence into Language and Action" by Audre Lorde

I want to thank Dustin Brookshire, who encouraged me to submit this manuscript to Harbor Editions, as well as Kristiane Weeks-Rogers who not only reviewed my first published choreopoem, *How to Exterminate the Black Woman*, but also accepted this choreopoem for publication. Shout out to the whole team!

Thank you, Laura Newbern, who introduced me to both Oulipian constraints and Bhanu Kapil.

Thanks to Steve Gibson for the gorgeous cover photos, and Hercules Platts for the incredible cover design work.

Thanks as always to Ntozake Shange for creating the choreopoem genre, and to all other practitioners of this form, especially Anya Pearson, Bryan-Keyth Wilson, and jessica Care moore. And thanks to Susquehanna University and the Writers Institute for giving me resources to teach choreopoems to students the world over.

Thank you to my family, my husband Rob, my polycule, my friends, and my therapist for all your continued support.

Curses and inconveniences to every person who raped me or anyone else. May you never find peace.

And finally, thanks to Barrelhouse's Writer Camp, where I first drafted this choreopoem and where I ultimately finished it. Special shout out to Halsey Hyer and Ty Phelps who read this before it went to print, to Dave Housley who brought me meals while I was in the zone completing this, and all past and future Writer Camp alumni who inspired me to keep writing even though I was crying in the party barn. The literary community is the best community.

Monica Prince serves as an Associate Professor of Activist and Performance Writing and the Director of Africana Studies at Susquehanna University in Pennsylvania. She is the author of four collections, most recently *Roadmap: A Choreopoem* (Santa Fe Writers Project, 2023) and *How to Exterminate the Black Woman: A Choreopoem* ([PANK] Books, 2020). Her poems and essays appear in national and international literary journals. As one of the foremost choreopoem scholars, Prince writes, teaches, and performs choreopoems across the nation. She shares her life with her husband, life partners, and three disrespectful cats. Check out her website: www.monicaprince.com.

About Small Harbor Publishing

Small Harbor Publishing is a 501c3 nonprofit organization. Our goal is to publish unique and diverse voices. We are a feminist press, and we are committed to diversity and inclusion. We strive to bring new voices to a devoted and expanding readership.

Small Harbor Publishing began in 2018 with the first issue of *Harbor Review*. The magazine is an online space where poetry and art converse. *Harbor Review* quickly grew and now publishes reviews and runs multiple micro chapbook competitions, including the Washburn Prize and the Editor's Prize.

In July 2020, Small Harbor Publishing was officially incorporated and began Harbor Editions. Harbor Editions accepts submissions through a chapbook open reading period, a hybrid chapbook open reading period, the Marginalia Series, and the Laureate Prize.

In 2023, Harbor Anthologies began with a mission to promote texts that explore social justice issues and highlight marginalized writers.

If you would like to support Small Harbor Publishing, visit our "About" page at: smallharborpublishing.com/about.

www.ingramcontent.com/pod-product-compliance
Lightning Source LLC
Chambersburg PA
CBHW030509130626
46549CB00007B/2909